HEROES
of CHINA

THE FIRST EMPEROR

OF CHINA

中国的第一个皇帝

JILLIAN LIN

Illustrations by SHI MENG

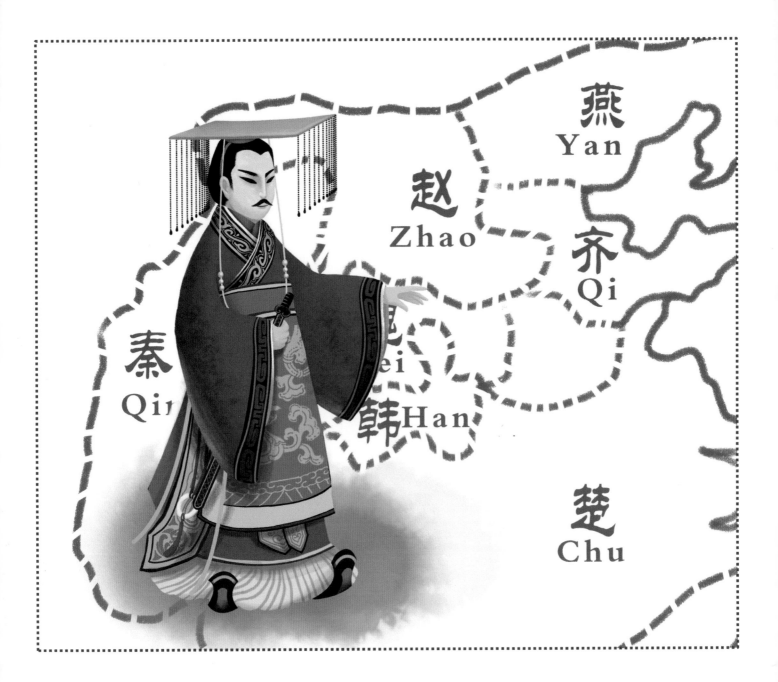

This is Chin.

He has an army of soldiers.

His soldiers take over China.

Chin becomes its first emperor.

这 是 秦,
他 有 一 只 军 队。
他 的 士 兵 占 领 了 全 中 国,
秦 成 为 中 国 的 第 一 个 皇 帝。

Chin builds roads and rivers.

He makes special coins.

People learn to write Chinese.

China becomes a better place.

秦 修 建 了 道 路 河 流，
他 制 造 了 特 殊 的 钱 币。
人 们 开 始 学 习 汉 语，
中 国 成 为 一 个 好 地 方。

One day, bad people attack China.

What can Chin do?

He has an idea.

'Let's build a wall,' he says.

一 天, 坏 人 攻 打 中 国,
秦 能 做 什 么 呢?
他 有 一 个 主 意,
"让 我 们 修 建 一 面 墙" 他 说。

Lots of people work on the wall.

It is hard work.

But the wall keeps bad people out.

China is safe again.

很 多 人 在 墙 上 工 作 着，
这 是 一 项 很 难 的 工 作。
但 是 墙 可 以 挡 住 敌 人，
中 国 再 一 次 安 全 了。

Chin has a wish.

'I want to live forever,' he says.

What if his wish does not come true?

Stone soldiers will keep him safe.

秦 有 一 个 心 愿，
"我 想 长 生 不 老" 他 说。
假 如 他 的 心 愿 不 能 实 现 呢？
石 头 士 兵 们 将 会 让 他 安 全。

Chin hears about a special drink.

It will make him live forever.

He goes on a trip to find it.

Sea monsters try to stop him.

秦 听 说 了 一 种 特 殊 的 药，
它 可 以 让 他 长 生 不 老。
他 四 处 去 寻 找 它，
海 怪 试 着 阻 止 他。

Chin does not find the drink.

His wish does not come true.

But in a way, Chin gets to live forever.

His name is in the word 'China'.

秦 没 有 找 到 药,
他 的 心 愿 没 有 实 现。
但 是 应 该 说, 他 一 直 活 着,
他 的 名 字 "秦" 就 在 "China" 中。

The End

The Great Wall is not one long wall, but it is made up of different parts.

Why do you think the wall was so hard to build?

长城不是一面长墙,而是由不同的部分组成。

你认为这墙为什么这么难建造呢?

Qin's stone soldiers looked like real people and took a long time to make.

How do the soldiers in the picture look different from one another?

秦 的 石 头 兵 看 起 来 象 真 人，花 了 很 长 时 间 制 作。

在 图 中 的 士 兵 如 何 看 起 来 彼 此 不 同？

KIRGHIZSTAN

AJIKISTAN

CASHMIR

THE GREAT WALL

CHINA

QIN BORDER ————

NEPAL

BHUTAN

INDIA

INDIA

MYANMAR

THE GREAT WALL

NORTH KOREA

BEIJING

SOUTH KOREA

CAPITAL CITY OF QIN

XIANYANG

XI'AN

SHANGHAI

FIRST EMPEROR'S TOMB

TAIWAN

HONG KONG

PACIFIC OCEAN

Books by Jillian Lin

The *Heroes Of China* Series (2-5 years) - English & 中文

Qin Shihuang (秦始皇)

Confucius (孔子)

Zhu Zaiyu (朱載堉)

Hua Tuo (华佗)

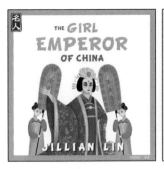

Wu Zetian (武则天)

Zhang Heng (張衡)

Zheng He (郑和)

Koxinga (國姓爺)

Also available as e-books. For more information, visit

www.jillianlin.com

The *Once Upon A Time In China* Series (6+ years) - English

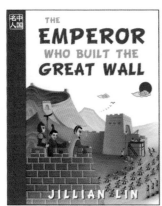

Qin Shihuang

Confucius

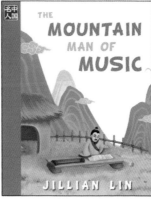

Zhu Zaiyu

Hua Tuo

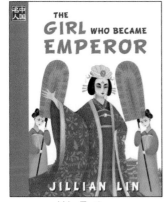

Wu Zetian

Zhang Heng

Zheng He

Koxinga

The First Emperor Of China

24296062R00016

Printed in Poland
by Amazon Fulfillment
Poland Sp. z o.o., Wrocław